ELSE**WHERE**

Harriet Monroe Poetry Institute

Poets in the World series editor

Ilya Kaminsky

ELSE**WHERE**

Edited by Eliot Weinberger

POETRY
FOUNDATION

OPEN LETTER
LITERARY TRANSLATIONS FROM THE UNIVERSITY OF ROCHESTER

POETRY

FOUNDATION

Elsewhere *is a publication of the Poetry Foundation and Open Letter.*
This book is published as part of the Poets in the World series created
by the Poetry Foundation's Harriet Monroe Poetry Institute.

Elsewhere : edited by Eliot Weinberger ; translated from the various languages by
Eliot Weinberger and others. — First edition.
    pages cm. — (Poets in the world)
    ISBN-13: 978-1-934824-85-6 (pbk. : alk. paper)
    ISBN-10: 1-934824-85-2 (pbk. : alk. paper)
    1. Poetry—Collections. 2. Poetry—Translations into English. I. Weinberger, Eliot,
editor of compilation.
    PN6101.E47 2013
    808.81—dc23
                                2013030302

Printed on acid-free paper in the United States of America. Text set in Jenson Pro, an old-style
serif typeface drawn by Robert Slimbach, based on a Venetian face cut by Nicolas Jenson in 1470.
Design by N. J. Furl

Open Letter is the University of Rochester's nonprofit, literary translation press:
Lattimore Hall 411, Box 270082, Rochester, NY 14627 | www.openletterbooks.org

"The Poetry Foundation" and the Pegasus logo are registered trademarks of the Poetry Foundation.
For more information about the Poetry Foundation: www.poetryfoundation.org

CONTENTS

ELSE**WHERE**

In a century of mass migration and deportation, political exile and casual tourism, being elsewhere was the common condition. For the moderns, elsewhere was not merely physical location or dislocation, but was intrinsic to the work. Victor Segalen, in China at the beginning of the century, writes of the "manifestation of Diversity," a "spectacle of Difference": everything that is "foreign, strange, unexpected, surprising, mysterious, amorous, superhuman, heroic, and even divine, everything that is *Other*." Picasso put it more bluntly: "Strangeness is what we wanted to make people think about because we were quite aware that our world was becoming very strange." After Guillaume Apollinaire's "Zone"—perhaps the most influential poem of the century—collage, the juxtaposition of disparate elements, the manifestation of diversity, the making of the strange, became the primary new form of the new poetry.

From the countless examples, here are a few instances of the collage of a poet pasted, physically or mentally, onto a specific unfamiliar landscape.

I. PARIS

The received wisdom is that Paris was the capital of the nineteenth century and New York of the twentieth. The demarcation, however, is not strictly calendrical. Paris remained the center of the new at least through the 1920s—and long after that for many in the rest of the world. For an Asian or a Latin American, Paris was the central station for the pilgrimage to world culture.

CATHEDRAL IN THE THRASHING RAIN
by Kōtarō Takamura (translated by Hiroaki Sato)

O another deluge of wind and rain.
Collar turned up, getting drenched in this splashing rain,
and looking up at you—it's me,
me who never fails to come here once a day.
It's that Japanese.
This morning
about daybreak the storm suddenly went violent, terrible,
and now is blowing through Paris from one end to the other.
I have yet to know the directions of this land.
I don't even know which way this storm is facing, raging over the
    Île-de-France.
Only because even today I wanted to stand here
and look up at you, Cathedral of Notre-Dame de Paris,
I came, getting drenched,
only because I wanted to touch you,
only because I wanted to kiss your skin, the stone, unknown to
    anyone.

O another deluge of wind and rain.
Though it's already time for morning coffee,
a little while ago I looked from the Pont-Neuf,
the boats on the Seine were still tied up to the banks, like puppies.
The leaves of the gentle plane trees shining in their autumn colors
    on the banks
are like flocks of buntings chased by hawks,
glittering, scattering, flying about.

The chestnut trees behind you,
each time their heads, spreading branches, get mussed up,
starling-colored leaves dance up into the sky.
By the splashes of rain blowing down, they are then
dashed like arrows on the cobblestones and burst.
All the square is like a pattern,
filled with flowing silver water, and isles of golden-brown burnt-
brown leaves.
Then there's the noise of the downpour resounding in my pores.
It's the noise of something roaring, grinding.
As soon as human beings hushed up
all the other things in Paris began at once to shout in chorus.
With golden plane tree leaves falling all over my coat,
I'm standing in it.
Storms are like this in my country, Japan, too.
Only, we don't see you soaring.

O Notre-Dame, Notre-Dame,
rock-like, mountain-like, eagle-like, crouching-lion-like cathedral,
reef sunk in vast air,
square pillar of Paris,
sealed by the blinding splatters of rain,
taking the slapping wind head-on,
O soaring in front, Notre-Dame de Paris,
it's me, looking up at you.
It's that Japanese.
My heart trembles now that I see you.
Looking at your form like a tragedy,
a young man from a far distant country is moved.
Not at all knowing for what reason, my heart pounds
in unison with the screams in the air, resounds as if terrified.

O another deluge of wind and rain.
How furious these four elements of nature
that would, if they could, snuff out your existence, return you to the
     original void.
Smoking phosphorescent shafts of rain.
Scales of the clouds flying, mottled, not quite touching your top.
Blasts of the persistent clinging gales, trying to snap off at least one
     column of the bell-tower.
Innumerable, small, shining elves that bump against the rose
     window dentils, burst, flow, and flap about.
Only the gargoyles, the monsters on the high architectural rims,
     visible between splashes,
taking on the flitting flocks of elves,
raise their paws, crane their necks,
bare their teeth, blow out burning fountains of breath.
The many lines of mysterious stone saints make eerie gestures, nod
     to one another
the enormous arc-boutants on the side reveal their familiar upper
     arms.
To their many arms that form arcs aslant,
O what a concentration of wind and rain.
I hear the reverberation of the organ during Mass
How is the rooster at the tip of the tall slender steeple doing?
Flapping curtains of water have dammed up all directions.
You stand in them.

O another deluge of wind and rain.
A cathedral standing in it
solid with the weight of eight centuries,
a mass of many millions of stones piled and carved by believers of old.
A great scaffold for truth, sincerity, and eternity.

You stand wordless,
you stand, taking on, motionless, the force of the blasting storm.
You know the strength of nature's force,
have the composure of mind to leave yourself to the rampant wind
    and rain, till the earth shakes.
O rusty gray iron-colored skin of stone glistening in the rain.
My hands touching it
feel as if they were touching Esmeralda's white palm.
And along with Esmeralda, the monster
Quasimodo who delights in storms is hiding near some molding.
A just soul crammed into an ugly body,
a firm strength,
silently absorbing on his back
the words of those who wounded, those who whipped, those who
    would do wrong, those who despised, and not to say the least,
    those who were petty,
he ground himself to serve God,
O only you could give birth to that monster.
How many non-hunchbacked, non-deformed, more joyful, more
    daily Quasimodos
have been born since then
and nurtured on your breast full of solemn, yet protective motherly
    love, and gentle.

O Cathedral in the thrashing rain.
Baton swung down abruptly at the sudden
turn of the wind and rain that took a breath and has driven itself
    harder,
all the instruments of the heavens gone berserk,
the dance swirls around them.

O Cathedral, you who at such a moment keep ever more silent and
    soar,
Cathedral, you who watch motionless the houses of Paris suffering
    the storm,
please do not think me rude,
who, hands on your cornerstone,
has his hot cheek pressed on your skin,
it's me, the drunken one.
It's that Japanese.

Enamored with Rodin, Kōtarō Takamura (1883-1956) went to Paris in 1908 to study sculpture, stayed a year, and never got over it. He returned to Tokyo to live a life of "French" bohemianism as both a sculptor and a poet. One of the greatest Japanese poets of the century, he is best known for two book-length sequences, *Chieko*, which recounts his wife's descent into schizophrenia, and *A Brief History of Imbecility*, where he relates and recants his enthusiastic nationalism during the Second World War. A poet of provincial and racial shame, his poem "The Country of Netsuke" ends: "small & frigid, incredibly smug / monkey-like, fox-like, flying-squirrel-like, mudskipper-like, minnow-like, gargoyle-like, chip-from-a-cup-like Japanese." A cultural inferiority complex that led him to flee to, then flee from, Paris; to support the war, then regret that he had done so.

EIFFEL TOWER

by Vicente Huidobro (translated by Eliot Weinberger)

for Robert Delaunay

Tour Eiffel
Guitare du ciel
Guitar of the sky

> Attracting words
> to your telegraphy
> like a rosebush its bees

At night
the Seine stops flowing

> Telescope or bugle

EIFFEL TOWER

It's a hive of words
an inkwell of honey

At the end of dawn
a spider with wire legs
spun a web of clouds

> My boy
> to climb the Eiffel Tower
> you climb up on a song

Do
re
mi
fa
so
la
ti
do

Nous sommes en haut
We're at the top

A bird sings	It's the wind
in the telegraph	of Europe
antennas	the electric wind

Hats fly off
They have wings but can't sing

Jacqueline
Daughter of France
What do you see up there?

The Seine's asleep
under the shadow of its bridges

I can see the Earth turning
and I blow my bugle
to all the seas

On the road
of your perfume
all the bees and all the words take off

On the four horizons
who hasn't heard this song

I AM THE QUEEN OF THE DAWN OF THE POLES
I AM THE COMPASS ROSE OF THE WINDS THAT
   FADES EVERY FALL
AND FILLED WITH SNOW
I DIE FROM THE DEATH OF THAT ROSE
ALL YEAR LONG A BIRD SINGS INSIDE MY HEAD

That's how the Tower spoke to me one day

Eiffel Tower
        Aviary of the world
                    Sing   Sing

Bell-clang of Paris

The giant hanging in the void
is a poster for France

                    On the day of Victory
                    you'll tell it to the stars

The Chilean poet Vicente Huidobro (1893-1948) is one of the few poets of the century whose life deserves a fat biography, which has never been written. In the thick of modernist "isms," he created his own—Creationism—of which he was the only member, and which instructed poets not to sing of the rose, but to make it bloom in the poem. He collaborated or fought with nearly everyone in the international avant-garde, participated in the Irish Liberation and the Spanish Civil War, made paintings of his poems, was a screenwriter in Hollywood, a candidate for president in Chile, and never recovered from the wounds he received as a correspondent in the Second World War. His book-length poem of an "antipoet" hurtling through Einsteinian space, *Altazor*, is surely the fastest-reading, most entertaining long poem of modernism.

He wrote in both Spanish and French (and occasionally English)—sometimes writing the same poem in both of his primary languages, so it becomes unclear which is the "original" and which the "translation." "Eiffel Tower," inspired by the paintings of Robert Delaunay, was written during World War I in French, and this translation attempts to play, as Huidobro often did, with his bilingualism.

20

A MAN FROM ECUADOR
BENEATH THE EIFFEL TOWER

by Jorge Carrera Andrade (translated by Thomas Merton)

You turn into a plant on the coasts of time
With your goblet of round sky,
Your opening for the tunnels of traffic.
You are the biggest ceiba tree on earth.

Up go the painter's eyes
By your scissor-stair, into the blue.

Over a flock of roofs
You stretch your neck, a llama of Peru.

Robed in folds of winds,
A comb of constellations in your hair,
You show yourself
To the circus of horizons.

Mast of an adventure above time!
Pride of five hundred and thirty cubits.

Pole of the tent set up by men
In a corner of history,
Your gaslit drawing in the night
Copies the milky way.

First letter of a cosmic alphabet,
Pointing in the direction of heaven,
Hope standing on stilts,
Glorification of the skeleton.

Iron to brand the flock of clouds
Or dumb sentinel of the industrial age.
The tides of heaven
Silently undermine your pillar.

A high-ranking diplomat and politician who went from post to post all over the world, Jorge Carrera Andrade (1902-1978) was, in the 1940s, the Latin American poet best known in the United States. Williams and Stevens, among many others, were enthusiasts. Today he is largely forgotten, though there have been some recent attempts to revive interest in his work. A universal poet might see the Eiffel Tower as a giant letter A—the first letter of the language of the future—but only an Andean would see it as a llama. And, after reading the poem, the unlikely llama remains a permanent component of what otherwise is an image of technological wonder. Poetry has this way of always going back to some Eden.

II. NEW YORK

In the city of perpetual immigration, there's no end of poems written by foreigners in New York. These are merely two of the better-known examples. But the perennial condition of the poet in New York, the anonymous watcher of the crowds, was perhaps best summed up in 1918 in a couplet by the Mexican José Juan Tablada:

> Mujeres que pasaís por la Quinta Avenida,
> tan cerca de mis ojos, tan lejos de mi vida . . .

[You women who walk on Fifth Avenue, / so near to my eyes, so far from my life . . .]

THE DAWN

by Federico García Lorca (translated by Eliot Weinberger)

Dawn in New York
is four pillars of sludge
and a hurricane of black pigeons
fluttering rank water.

Dawn in New York
howls through the stairwells,
searching the jagged angles
for spikenards of sketched affliction.

Dawn comes and no one welcomes it in his mouth,
for there's no morning, no hope possible there,
and at times the angry swarms of coins
drill and devour abandoned kids.

The first ones out know in their bones
there'll be no paradise, no love unleafing;
they know they're going to a slough of figures and rules,
games without skill, sweat without fruit.

The light is buried under chains and clangor,
threatened openly by rootless science.
There are people staggering sleepless through the boroughs
as though they've just escaped a shipwreck of blood.

Federico García Lorca (1898-1936) came to New York in 1929, in time to witness the stock market crash. He stayed for a year. His book *Poet in New York*, a masterpiece of this "elsewhere" genre, was first published posthumously in the United States in 1942. (It would never have been allowed in Franco's Spain.) From the first line of the first poem—"Assassinated by the sky"—one is sunk in a nightmare of dislocation otherwise only found in the poems of soldiers, prisoners, or refugees.

NEW YORK
(TRUMPET SOLO FOR JAZZ ORCHESTRA)
by Léopold Sédar Senghor (translated by Ellen Conroy Kennedy)

1

New York! At first I was confounded by your beauty, those tall
long-legged golden girls.
Timid at first before your metallic blue eyes, your frosty smile,
So timid, and my anguish at the bottom of your skyscraping streets,
raising owl-eyes toward the blacked-out sun.
Sulfurous your light and the livid shafts whose heads smash up
against the sky.
Skyscrapers whose steely muscle and bronzed stony skin challenge
cyclones.
Fifteen days on Manhattan's naked sidewalks
—at the third week's end the fever grabs one with a jaguar's leap,
Fifteen days without wellspring or pasture, birds falling suddenly
dead from sooty rooftops.
No blossoming child's laughter, his hand in my cool one.
No maternal breast, nyloned legs. Legs and breasts without odor or
sweat.
No tender word in the absence of lips, nothing but artificial hearts
paid for at high prices.
And no book in which to read wisdom. The painter's palette is
bedecked with coral crystals.
O insomniac Manhattan nights! So stirred up with lively lights,
while auto horns blare forth the empty hours
And murky waters carry past hygienic loves, like flood rivers, the
bodies of dead children.

2

Now is the season for the renderings and accounts,
New York! Yes, now is the time for manna and hyssop.
Only listen to God's trombones, let your heart beat to the rhythm
    of blood, your blood.
I have seen in Harlem, humming with sounds, ceremonious colors
    and flamboyant scents
—at teatime in the drugstores.
I have seen the festival of night in preparation at the flight of day. I
    proclaim the night more truthful than the day.
This is the pure hour when God makes immemorial life spring
    forth in the streets,
Its amphibious elements radiating like suns.
Harlem! Harlem! This is what I've seen—Harlem, Harlem!
A green breeze of wheat springing from pavements plowed by
    barefoot dancers waving silken rumps and spearhead breasts,
    ballets of waterlilies and fabulous masks.
At the feet of police horses, the mangoes of love rolling from low
    houses.
And I have seen along the sidewalks rivulets of white rum, rivulets
    of black milk in the blue fog of cigars.
I have seen snowfalls at night of cotton flowers, seraphic wings and
    sorcerers' plumes.
Listen, New York! Oh listen to your virile, copper voice, your
    vibrating oboe's voice, hear the stopped-up anguish of your tears
    fall in great clots of blood.
Hear the distant beat of your nocturnal heart, rhythm and blood of
    the tom-tom, tom-tom blood and tom-tom.

3

New York! I say New York, let black blood flow in your blood,

Let it rub the rust from your steely joints, like a life-giving oil

Till it gives your bridges the curves of buttocks and the suppleness
of vines.

For then will be refound the unity of ancient times, the
reconciliation of Lion, Bull, and Tree,

Idea linked to act, ear to heart, and sign to sense.

There are your rivers rippling with musky crocodiles and mirage-
eyed manatees. And no need to invent any Sirens.

But it is enough to behold an April rainbow

And to hear, especially to hear the Lord, who with a saxophonic
laugh, created heaven and earth in six days.

And on the seventh, slept a great Negro sleep.

Harlem in the 1920s and 1930s may well have been, at the time, the most important cultural nexus and symbol of the modern. It was the source of the new universal sound for the new age: jazz. Europeans, sick of European culture and longing to return to some imaginary roots, saw it as the place for a human vitality that had been lost to the etiolated bourgeoisie. Black writers and artists considered it the center of a new culture and a new consciousness that would span the African diaspora. Léopold Sédar Senghor (1906-2001) would later coin the name for this consciousness for the Francophone world: *négritude*. Senghor was a major theoretician, internationally the best-known African poet of the century, and the president of his native Senegal. He is surely the only modern poet for whom an airport is named.

III. LOS ANGELES

Los Angeles, the city that was once unlike any other city and yet was not quite the City of the Future, was oddly inspirational in the 1930s and 1940s.

L.A. NOCTURNE: THE ANGELS

by Xavier Villaurrutia (translated by Eliot Weinberger)

for Agustín J. Fink

You might say the streets flow sweetly through the night.
The lights are dim so the secret will be kept,
the secret known by the men who come and go,
for they're all in on the secret
and why break it up in a thousand pieces
when it's so sweet to hold it close,
and share it only with the one chosen person.

If, at a given moment, everyone would say
with one word what he is thinking,
the six letters of DESIRE would form an enormous luminous scar,
a constellation more ancient, more dazzling than any other.
And that constellation would be like a burning sex
in the deep body of night,
like the Gemini, for the first time in their lives,
looking each other in the eyes and embracing forever.

Suddenly the river of the street is filled with thirsty creatures;
they walk, they pause, they move on.
They exchange glances, they dare to smile,
they form unpredictable couples . . .

There are nooks and benches in the shadows,
riverbanks of dense indefinable shapes,

sudden empty spaces of blinding light
and doors that open at the slightest touch.

For a moment, the river of the street is deserted.
Then it seems to replenish itself,
eager to start again.
It is a paralyzed, mute, gasping moment,
like a heart between two spasms.

But a new throbbing, a new pulsebeat
launches new thirsty creatures on the river of the street.
They cross, crisscross, fly up.
They glide along the ground.
They swim standing up, so miraculously
no one would ever say they're not really walking.

They are angels.
They have come down to earth
on invisible ladders.
They come from the sea that is the mirror of the sky
on ships of smoke and shadow,
they come to fuse and be confused with men,
to surrender their foreheads to the thighs of women,
to let other hands anxiously touch their bodies
and let other bodies search for their bodies till they're found,
like the closing lips of a single mouth,
they come to exhaust their mouths, so long inactive,
to set free their tongues of fire,
to sing the songs, to swear, to say all the bad words
in which men have concentrated the ancient mysteries
of flesh, blood and desire.

They have assumed names that are divinely simple.
They call themselves *Dick* or *John*, *Marvin* or *Louis*.
Only by their beauty are they distinguishable from men.
They walk, they pause, they move on.
They exchange glances, they dare to smile.
They form unpredictable couples.

They smile maliciously going up in the elevators of hotels,
where leisurely vertical flight is still practiced.
There are celestial marks on their naked bodies:
blue signs, blue stars and letters.
They let themselves fall into beds, they sink into pillows
that make them think they're still in the clouds.
But they close their eyes to surrender to the pleasures of their
    mysterious incarnation,
and when they sleep, they dream not of angels but of men.

The Mexican poet Xavier Villaurrutia (1903-1950) was one of the few writers in the first half of the century who was openly gay and whose homoerotic lyrics are worth reading alongside those of Constantine Cavafy. He essentially wrote one book of poems, *Nostalgia for Death*, first published in 1938 and then expanded in 1946. After that, he turned to drawing-room comedies for the Mexican stage. Octavio Paz, in a book-length study of Villaurrutia, wrote that his poetry "seems to have been written not only in some other country, but in a place beyond geography and history, beyond myth and legend, a nowhere that 'occupies no place in space,' in which time has stopped."

HOLLYWOOD ELEGIES

by Bertolt Brecht (translated by John Willett)

I
The village of Hollywood was planned according to the notion
People in these parts have of heaven. In these parts
They have come to the conclusion that God
Requiring a heaven and a hell, didn't need to
Plan two establishments but
Just the one: heaven. It
Serves the unprosperous, unsuccessful
As hell.

II
By the sea stand the oil derricks. Up the canyons
The gold prospectors' bones lie bleaching. Their sons
Built the dream factories of Hollywood.
The four cities
Are filled with the oily smell
Of films.

III
The city is named after the angels
And you meet angels on every hand.
They smell of oil and wear golden pessaries
And, with blue rings round their eyes
Feed the writers in their swimming pools every morning.

IV
Beneath the green pepper trees
The musicians play the whore, two by two
With the writers. Bach
Has written a Strumpet Voluntary. Dante wriggles
His shriveled bottom.

V
The angels of Los Angeles
Are tired out with smiling. Desperately
Behind the fruit stalls of an evening
They buy little bottles
Containing sex odours.

VI
Above the four cities the fighter planes
Of the Defense Department circle at a great height
So that the stink of greed and poverty
Shall not reach them.

Bertolt Brecht (1898-1956), escaping the Nazis, moved to Los Angeles in 1941, where he became part of a German exile community that included, among many others, Thomas Mann, Arnold Schoenberg, and Alfred Döblin—unimaginable in the land of Mickey Rooney and Mickey Mouse. He left in 1947, after testifying before the House Un-American Activities committee, in what has come to be considered a classic befuddlement of a righteous bureaucracy.

In the late 1930s, Charles Reznikoff—who otherwise almost never left New York—spent two years in Hollywood, ostensibly working as a screenwriter for his childhood friend, the producer Albert Lewin. Reznikoff had nothing to do and writes of watching the flies on his desk. One of the poems in his sequence "Autobiography: Hollywood" reads:

> It has been raining for three days.
> The faces of the giants
> on the bill-boards
> still smile,
> but the gilt has been washed from the sky:
> we see the iron world.

IV. TRAINS & CARS

Modernist poetry celebrated the new age of speed embodied in airplanes and motor cars, but poems about actual journeys tended to be written on or about nineteenth century modes of transportation: ships and trains. The automobile, particularly in the car culture of the United States, lent itself more to prose narrative, the stories of being on the road. An airplane trip, after the first decades, was too removed from actual experience, unless one was a pilot (and only a few poets in the Second World War were pilots). The best sequence about airplanes remains Muriel Rukeyser's first book, *Theory of Flight* (1935). Two of the greatest poems of, respectively, trains and ships are too long to be included here: Blaise Cendrars's 1913 "The Prose of the Trans-Siberian and of Little Jeanne of France" and the 1924 "The *Formosa*" sequence from his book *Travel Notes*.

THINGS I DIDN'T KNOW I LOVED

by Nâzim Hikmet (translated by Randy Blasing & Mutlu Konuk)

it's 1962 March 28th
I'm sitting by the window on the Prague-Berlin train
night is falling
I never knew I liked
night descending like a tired bird on a smoky wet plain
I don't like
comparing nightfall to a tired bird

I didn't know I loved the earth
can someone who hasn't worked the earth love it
I've never worked the earth
it must be my only Platonic love

and here I've loved rivers all this time
whether motionless like this they curl skirting the hills
European hills crowned with chateaus
or whether stretched out flat as far as the eye can see
I know you can't wash in the same river even once
I know the river will bring new lights you'll never see
I know we live slightly longer than a horse but not nearly as long as
    a crow
I know this has troubled people before
                     and will trouble those after me
I know all this has been said a thousand times before
                     and will be said after me

I didn't know I loved the sky
cloudy or clear
the blue vault Andrei studied on his back at Borodino
in prison I translated both volumes of *War and Peace* into Turkish
I hear voices
not from the blue vault but from the yard
the guards are beating someone again

I didn't know I loved trees
bare beeches near Moscow in Peredelkino
they come upon me in winter noble and modest
beeches are Russian the way poplars are Turkish
"the poplars of Izmir
losing their leaves . . .
they call me The Knife . . .
                              lover like a young tree . . .
I blow stately mansions sky-high"
in the Ilgaz woods in 1920 I tied an embroidered linen handkerchief
                              to a pine bough for luck

I never knew I loved roads
even the asphalt kind
Vera's behind the wheel we're driving from Moscow to the Crimea
                              Koktebele
                    formerly "Goktepé ili" in Turkish
the two of us inside a closed box
the world flows past on both sides distant and mute
I was never so close to anyone in my life
bandits stopped me on the red road between Bolu and Geredé
                              when I was eighteen

apart from my life I didn't have anything in the wagon they could
    take
and at eighteen our lives are what we value least
I've written this somewhere before
wading through a dark muddy street I'm going to the shadow play
Ramazan night
a paper lantern leading the way
maybe nothing like this ever happened
maybe I read it somewhere an eight-year-old boy
                                        going to the shadow play
Ramazan night in Istanbul holding his grandfather's hand
    his grandfather has on a fez and is wearing the fur coat
        with a sable collar over his robe
    and there's a lantern in the servant's hand
    and I can't contain myself for joy

flowers come to mind for some reason
poppies cactuses jonquils
in the jonquil garden in Kadikoy Istanbul I kissed Marika
fresh almonds on her breath
I was seventeen
my heart on a swing touched the sky
I didn't know I loved flowers
friends sent me three red carnations in prison

I just remembered the stars
I love them too
whether I'm floored watching them from below
or whether I'm flying at their side

I have some questions for the cosmonauts
were the stars much bigger
did they look like huge jewels on black velvet
                              or apricots on orange
did you feel proud to get closer to the stars
I saw color photos of the cosmos in *Ogonek* magazine now don't
    be upset comrades but nonfigurative shall we say or abstract
    well some of them looked just like such paintings which is to
    say they were terribly figurative and concrete
my heart was in my mouth looking at them
they are our endless desire to grasp things
seeing them I could even think of death and not feel at all sad
I never knew I loved the cosmos

snow flashes in front of my eyes
both heavy wet steady snow and the dry whirling kind
I didn't know I liked snow

I never knew I loved the sun
even when setting cherry-red as now
in Istanbul too it sometimes sets in postcard colors
but you aren't about to paint it that way

I didn't know I loved the sea
                              except the Sea of Azov
or how much

I didn't know I loved clouds
whether I'm under or up above them
whether they look like giants or shaggy white beasts

moonlight the falsest the most languid the most petit-bourgeois
strikes me
I like it

I didn't know I liked rain
whether it falls like a fine net or splatters against the glass my
    heart leaves me tangled up in a net or trapped inside a drop
    and takes off for uncharted countries I didn't know I loved
    rain but why did I suddenly discover all these passions sitting
    by the window on the Prague-Berlin train
is it because I lit my sixth cigarette
one alone could kill me
is it because I'm half dead from thinking about someone back in
    Moscow
her hair straw-blond eyelashes blue

the train plunges on through the pitch-black night
I never knew I liked the night pitch-black
sparks fly from the engine
I didn't know I loved sparks
I didn't know I loved so many things and I had to wait until sixty
    to find it out sitting by the window on the Prague-Berlin train
    watching the world disappear as if on a journey of no return

19 April 1962
Moscow

Once one of the best-known poets in the world—a Communist who combined indignation at social injustice with a passionate celebration of ordinary things—the Turkish populist Nâzim Hikmet (1902-1963) spent more than half of his adult life—26 years—in prison or in exile. An international *cause célèbre*, everyone from Picasso to Sartre joined in the campaign to free him from solitary confinement and torture. In this poem, written the year before he died, the passing landscape outside the train window leads, as it so often does, to a train of memories, a traversal of both space and time.

AT THE WHEEL OF THE CHEVROLET ON THE ROAD TO SINTRA

by Fernando Pessoa (as Álvaro de Campos)
(translated by Edwin Honig & Susan M. Brown)

At the wheel of the Chevrolet on the road to Sintra
Under moonlight and dream, on the deserted road,
I drive alone, slow and easy, and it seems to me
A bit—or I make myself think it so a bit—
That I'm following some other road, some other dream, some other
world,
I'm going on, not with Lisbon there behind or Sintra ahead,
I'm going on, and what more is there to it than not stopping, just
going on?

I'll be spending the night in Sintra, since I'm unable to spend it in
Lisbon.
But when I get to Sintra, I'll be sorry I'm not staying in Lisbon.
Always this restlessness, aimless, inconsequential, pointless,
Always, always, always,
The mind's excessive anguish over nothing at all,
On the Sintra highway, dream highway, life highway . . .

Responding to my subconscious motions at the wheel,
The car I borrowed moves like a greyhound with me and under me.
I smile as I think of the symbol, turning to the right.
So many borrowed things I go along with in this world!
So many borrowed things I drive on with as if they were mine!
What's been lent me, alas, is what I myself am!

To the left, a hovel—yes, a hovel—at the side of the road.
To the right, an open field and the moon in the distance.
The car, which just before seemed to offer me freedom,
Now becomes something I'm locked up in,
Something I can only control if I'm part of, if it's part of me.

Behind, to the left, there's the hovel and more than hovel.
Life must be happy there, simply because it isn't my life.
If someone saw me from the window, they'd imagine: there's
    someone who's happy.
Maybe to the child gazing through the panes of the top-story
    window
I was, like the borrowed car, a dream, an honest-to-goodness fairy.
Maybe to the girl hearing the motor who watched from the ground-
    floor kitchen window,
I'm a bit of the prince all girls dream about,
And through the panes she'll take me in sidelong till I vanish
    around the bend.
I'll leave dreams behind me—or is it the car that will?

I, the driver of a borrowed car, or I the borrowed car I drive?

On the road to Sintra and sad in the moonlight, with the night and
    fields before me,
Driving the borrowed Chevrolet, and miserable,
I lose myself on the road of things to come, vanish in the distance I
    am overtaking,
And out of some sudden, terrible, violent, incredible impulse,
I accelerate . . .
But I left my heart back there on that stone pile I steered clear of,

Seeing it without seeing it,
At the door to the hovel,
My empty heart,
My unappeased heart,
My heart, more human than I am, more precise than life.

On the road to Sintra, near midnight, at the wheel in the moonlight,
On the road to Sintra, tired of my own fancies,
On the road to Sintra, each moment closer to Sintra,
On the road to Sintra, each moment farther away from myself . . .

1928

After a childhood and adolescence in Durban, South Africa, Fernando Pessoa (1888-1935) never left Portugal and rarely ventured outside of Lisbon. This poem is the only one in this set that does not take place in a country foreign to the writer, but, written in 1928, it is surely one of the earliest poems about driving a car. Somehow it belongs alongside a photo by Jacques Henri Lartigue.

It has often been said that the greatest Portuguese poets of the twentieth century were all Fernando Pessoa. Following Whitman's exhortation for the poet to "contain multitudes," he created at least 72 heteronyms—each with a different biography, philosophy, style, and preoccupations. The author of this poem, Álvaro de Campos, was a naval engineer, formerly residing in Glasgow but now living in Lisbon, thin, quite tall but with a "tendency to stoop," hair "smooth and parted on the side, monocled." "On some holiday, he went to the Orient." There are some 25,000 pages of Pessoa manuscripts and no doubt further heteronyms will come to light.

V. IMAGINARY COUNTRIES

NORWAY

by Joaquín Pasos (translated by Eliot Weinberger)

Oh, this is Norway!
soft as cotton,
with its earth like cookies
and its coastline nibbled by the sea.

I've been on the bridge all morning,
the carts of fishmongers going by.
Every minute a rundown little window factory
tosses the red diabolo of a streetcar.

Oh, this is Norway,
with its metal trees
and its young ladies raised in refrigerators.
Here the birds whirl like windmills
and horses are more docile than in Holland.
The fjords go up like an old theater curtain
and the sun goes down every six months.

Fish-land towed by the Pole,
white bear with the green eye of Spitzbergen.
P-uuuuuu!

I've been on the bridge all evening,
the carts of fishmongers going by.
A dead cod falls from a truck
and is guillotined by a streetcar.

Oh, this is Norway!
green and white,
white and green like an old man:
obscene.

The Nicaraguan poet Joaquín Pasos was born in 1914—the same year as Octavio Paz, Nicanor Parra, and Julio Cortázar—but he only he lived until 1947, dying before his 33rd birthday. His one book of poems was published posthumously. Called *Poems of a Young Man*, its sections include "Poems of a Young Man Who Has Never Been in Love," which are all love poems; "Poems of a Young Man Who Does Not Speak English," which are all written in Pasos's idiosyncratic, self-taught English; and "Poems of a Young Man Who Has Never Traveled," which are, of course, travel poems. "Norway" comes from this last section. Pasos never left Nicaragua. By age 15, when this poem was written, he was already a pillar of the new Nicaraguan vanguard. Only a few of his poems have been translated.

GUINEA

by Jacques Roumain (translated by Langston Hughes)

It's the long road to Guinea
death takes you down.
Here are the boughs, the trees, the forest.
Listen to the sound of the wind in its long hair
    of eternal night.

It's the long road to Guinea
where your fathers await you without impatience.
Along the way, they talk,
They wait.
This is the hour when the streams rattle
    like beads of bone.

It's the long road to Guinea.
No bright welcome will be made for you
in the dark land of dark men:

Under a smoky sky pierced by the cry of birds
around the eye of the river
    the eyelashes of the trees open on decaying light.
There, there awaits you beside the water a quiet village,
and the hut of your fathers, and the hard ancestral stone
    where your head will rest at last.

A Haitian imagines Africa. Jacques Roumain (1907-1944), a poet, novelist, anthropologist, and Communist, was the leading Haitian intellectual of his time. Strangely, almost nothing is known of his life. He is considered part of the Negritude movement and was anthologized by Senghor, but it is not known whether he ever had any actual contact with any of its members. In 1927, he founded a magazine in Haiti called *La Revue indigène* (The Native Review), in part devoted to recuperating Haiti's African heritage. Langston Hughes found Roumain's poems there and translated them for the NAACP magazine, *The Crisis*. There is a book to be written about the network of poets that once existed across the African diaspora from the 1920s to the early 1970s, embracing such movements as Negritude and Black Nationalism, publishing and translating each other's work in magazines in Africa, the U.S., and the Caribbean—a neglected story in the history of international modernism.

OCEAN-LETTER

by Guillaume Apollinaire (translated by Anne Hyde Greet)

Ocean-Letter

nose in the air
I cross the city
and i cut it in 2

I was on the banks of the Rhine when you left for Mexico

Your voice reaches me in spite of the huge distance

Seedy-looking people on the pier at Vera Cruz

Since the travelers on the *Espagne* are supposed

to go to Coatzacoalcos in order to embark

I send you this card today instead

Juan Aldama

YPIRANGA

REPUBLICA MEXICANA

TARJETA POSTAL

11 45
29 – 5
14
Rue des Batignolles

of profiting by the Vera Cruz mails which aren't dependable

Everything is quiet here and we are awaiting events.

Correos
Mexico
4 centavos

U. S. Postage
2 cents 2

T S F

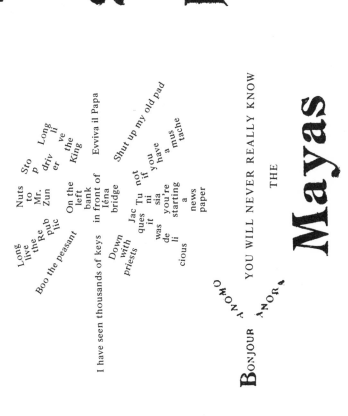

Long live the Republic

Boo the peasant

Nuts to Mr. Zun

Stop driver

Long live the King

Evviva il Papa

Shut up my old pad

I have seen thousands of keys

On the left bank in front of Iéna bridge

Down with priests

Jacques it was delicious

Tu ni sia you're starting a newspaper

not if you have a mustache

BONJOUR TOMMY

TONY

YOU WILL NEVER REALLY KNOW

THE

Mayas

Do you remember the earthquake between 1885 and 1890 people slept in tents for more than a month

HELLO MY BROTHER ALBERT in Mexico

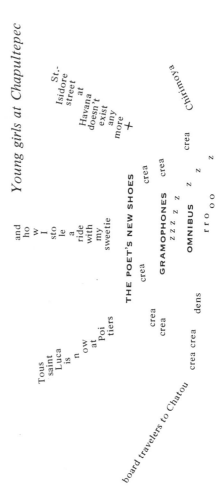

Young girls at Chapultepec

St.-
Isidore
street
at
Havana
doesn't
exist
any
more

Chirimoya

and
ho
w
I
sto
le
a
ride
with
my
sweetie

THE POET'S NEW SHOES

crea   crea   crea

GRAMOPHONES
z z z z z

OMNIBUS z z

crea

rr o o o   z

Tous
saint
Luca
is
n   ow
at
Poi
tiers

crea
crea

crea crea dens

board travelers to Chatou   crea crea

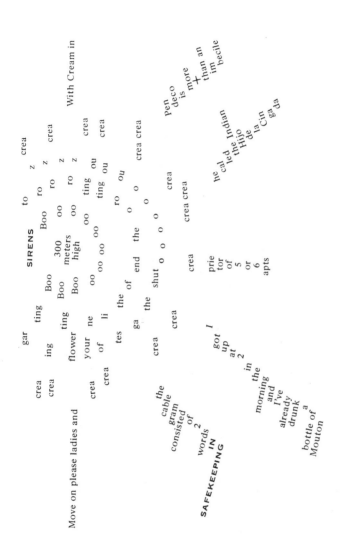

With Cream in

SIRENS to

crea

Boo ro z z z crea

300 meters high ting ou crea

Boo oo oo ting ou

Boo oo ro ou

gar ting ting ting Boo oo oo oo o o crea crea

ing flower your ne of li tes the of the ga end the shut o o o o crea crea

crea crea crea crea

Move on please ladies and

Pen deco is more + than an im becile

he cal led Indian the Hijo de la Cin ga da

prie tor of 5 or 6 apts

the cable gram consisted of 2 words

SAFEKEEPING IN

I got up at 2 in the morning and I've already drunk a bottle of a Mouton

An astonishing number of the practices of vanguardist poetry come from Guillaume Apollinaire (1880-1918): simultaneity, collage, automatic writing, surrealism (a term he invented) and, following Mallarmé's "Un coup de dès," a preoccupation with the arrangement of the words on the page, which he called "visual lyricism." He named his concrete poems "calligrams" (calligraphy + telegram) and they were immediately widely imitated. Some were pictorial (a poem about the rain in the shape of rain), others more abstract. Apollinaire, who never left Europe, died on the day World War I ended, from a combination of the Spanish Flu epidemic and the wounds he had received as a soldier.

The ocean-letter was devised a few years before this poem was written in 1914. On board ship, one wrote a message, which was relayed by shortwave radio to a ship going in the opposite direction. When the second ship landed, the message was mailed. The layout of words on the page could not, of course, be transmitted. Apollinaire's poem is not itself an ocean-letter, but an image of the system and the world of ocean-letters. The most visually complex of the calligrams, it portrays the babel of modern voices: radio waves emanating from the Eiffel Tower, the gramophone record that Apollinaire thought would replace printed poetry, scraps of old poems (including his own), bits of speech heard on the street, and actual letters, simultaneously to and from his brother Albert in Mexico.

Blaise Cendrars, some ten years later, wrote: "The ocean letter was not invented for writing poetry / But when you travel when you do business when you're on board when you send ocean letters / It's poetry" (trans. Ron Padgett).

THE WATER AND MONGOLIA

by Toriko Takarabe (translated by Hiroaki Sato)

When I drink water, I wouldn't think of the sea.
I just stand in my kitchen,
looking up at the dirty blue ventilator.

I wouldn't feel, in my mind or on my back,
estuaries, inlets, or roaring waves in the distance.
I wouldn't think
that in the Mongolian grassland that resembles a sea,
in a *pao* in its midst,
there, too, is a TV. I wouldn't think
that almost all of the human body is made of water.
I wouldn't think the soul is made of water.

When I drink water
a sheep runs down my windpipe
like a brush of pianissimo.
At that moment my healed flesh
will give itself a tremble.
But when the water passes down my throat,
I wouldn't think of a Mongolian man following his sheep.

When you drink water, you wouldn't think of
a Mongolian man, either.
You wouldn't think
that simply because the sound of your throat echoes,
the Mongolian man, in his long sheepskin boots,
walks down to the water's edge, in large strides.

Walk, walk, to where the water shines.
When a wind blows across the withered grassland along the water's
    edge,
the grass bends, flowing low, flowing low, just like sheep
asleep.
The withered grass rebels against the wind and stirs,
that quick, soft leap
of that stirring, moving sound! No, you wouldn't think of such a
    thing,
when the water passes down your throat.

Simply from a transparent glass
you drink water single-mindedly.
That's of course what you do.

Toriko Takarabe was born in Japan in 1933, but while she was a baby the family moved to Manchukuo, Japanese-occupied Manchuria. In the chaos at the end of the Second World War, one-fourth of the more than 300,000 Japanese immigrants died, including Takarabe's father and baby sister. She herself survived because her father had cut off all her hair to make her look a boy and prevent kidnaping and rape. She became a poet, novelist, and translator of Chinese. The glass of water that makes her think of Mongolia also leaps east across the Pacific to a major Mexican poem of the century: José Gorostiza's 1939 "Death Without End," a long philosophical mediation on—a glass of water. And then it leaps again to Scotland, to Hugh MacDiarmid's "The Glass of Pure Water"—one of those poems that, in three pages, seems to be about everything. Few of Takarabe's poems have been translated.

VI. CODA

From the great Austrian poet, Ingeborg Bachmann (1926-1973).

STAY

by Ingeborg Bachmann (translated by Peter Filkins)

Now the journey is ending,
the wind is losing heart.
Into your hands it's falling,
a rickety house of cards.

The cards are backed with pictures
displaying all the world.
You've stacked up all the images
and shuffled them with words.

And how profound the playing
that once again begins!
Stay, the card you're drawing
is the only world you'll win.

Eliot Weinberger is an essayist, poet, editor, and translator who won the National Book Critics Circle award for criticism for his edition of Jorge Luis Borges's *Selected Non-Fictions*. His translations of Octavio Paz are highly regarded, as are his translations of Homero Aridjis, Bei Dao, and many others. In addition to his translations, Weinberger is the author of *Nineteen Ways of Looking at Wang Wei, What Happened Here: Bush Chronicles, An Elemental Thing*, and several other essay collections.

Open Letter—the University of Rochester's nonprofit, literary translation press—is one of only a handful of publishing houses dedicated to increasing access to world literature for English readers. Publishing ten titles in translation each year, Open Letter searches for works that are extraordinary and influential, works that we hope will become the classics of tomorrow.

Making world literature available in English is crucial to opening our cultural borders, and its availability plays a vital role in maintaining a healthy and vibrant book culture. Open Letter strives to cultivate an audience for these works by helping readers discover imaginative, stunning works of fiction and poetry, and by creating a constellation of international writing that is engaging, stimulating, and enduring.

Current and forthcoming titles from Open Letter include works from Argentina, Bulgaria, Denmark, France, Germany, Latvia, Poland, Russia, and many other countries.

www.openletterbooks.org

Elsewhere is part of a collaboration with the *Poets in the World* series created by the Poetry Foundation's Harriet Monroe Poetry Institute. The *Poets in the World* series supports research and publication of poetry and poetics from around the world and highlights the importance of creating a space for poetry in local communities.

THE HARRIET MONROE POETRY INSTITUTE

is an independent forum created by the Poetry Foundation to provide a space in which fresh thinking about poetry, in both its intellectual and practical needs, can flourish free of allegiances other than to the best ideas. The Institute convenes leading poets, scholars, publishers, educators, and other thinkers from inside and outside the poetry world to address issues of importance to the art form of poetry and to identify and champion solutions for the benefit of the art. For more information, please visit www.poetryfoundation.org/institute.

The Poetry Foundation, publisher of *Poetry* magazine, is an independent literary organization committed to a vigorous presence for poetry in our culture. It exists to discover and celebrate the best poetry and to place it before the largest possible audience. The Poetry Foundation seeks to be a leader in shaping a receptive climate for poetry by developing new audiences, creating new avenues for delivery, and encouraging new kinds of poetry through innovative partnerships, prizes, and programs. For more information, please visit www.poetryfoundation.org.

Harriet Monroe Poetry Institute,
Poets in the World *Series*

Publications

Ilya Kaminsky, 2011-2013, HMPI director, Poets in the World *series editor*

Another English: Anglophone Poems from Around the World,
edited by Catherine Barnett and Tiphanie Yanique (Tupelo Press)

Elsewhere, edited by Eliot Weinberger (Open Letter Books)

Fifteen Iraqi Poets, edited by Dunya Mikhail (New Directions Publishing)

"Landays: Poetry of Afghan Women" edited by Eliza Griswold
(*Poetry* magazine, June 2013)

New Cathay: Contemporary Chinese Poetry, edited by Ming Di (Tupelo Press)

Open the Door: How to Excite Young People about Poetry, edited by
Dorothea Lasky, Dominic Luxford, and Jesse Nathan (McSweeney's)

Pinholes in the Night: Essential Poems from Latin America, edited by
Raúl Zurita and Forrest Gander (Copper Canyon Press)

Seven New Generation African Poets, edited by
Kwame Dawes and Chris Abani (Slapering Hol Press)

Something Indecent: Poems Recommended by Eastern European Poets,
edited by Valzhyna Mort (Red Hen Press)

The Star by My Head: Poets from Sweden, coedited and translated by
Malena Mörling and Jonas Ellerström (Milkweed Editions)

The Strangest of Theatres: Poets Writing Across Borders, edited by
Jared Hawkley, Susan Rich, and Brian Turner (McSweeney's)

Katharine Coles, HMPI inaugural director

Blueprints: Bringing Poetry into Communities, edited by
Katharine Coles (University of Utah Press)

Code of Best Practices in Fair Use for Poetry, created with American University's
Center for Social Media and Washington College of Law

Poetry and New Media: A Users' Guide, report of the Poetry and
New Media Working Group (Harriet Monroe Poetry Institute)